C00810460X

D0264680

LEISURE AND CULTURE DUNDEE	
C00810460X	
Bertrams	01/05/2019
	£7.99
CC	796.53

GO WILD
AT THE
SEASIDE

First published 2019 by Nosy Crow Ltd
The Crow's Nest, 14 Baden Place
Crosby Row, London, SE1 1YW
www.nosycrow.com

ISBN 978 1 78800 332 2

'The National Trust' and the oak leaf logo are registered
trademarks of the National Trust (Enterprises) Limited
(a subsidiary of The National Trust for Places of Historic Interest
or Natural Beauty, Registered Charity Number 205846).

Nosy Crow and associated logos are trademarks
and/or registered trademarks of Nosy Crow Ltd.

Text © Goldie Hawk 2019
Illustrations © Rachael Saunders 2019

The right of Goldie Hawk to be identified as the author and Rachael
Saunders to be identified as the illustrator of this work has been asserted.

All rights reserved.

This book is sold subject to the condition that it shall not, by way of trade or
otherwise, be lent, hired out or otherwise circulated in any form of binding
or cover other than that in which it is published. No part of this publication
may be reproduced, stored in a retrieval system, or transmitted in any
form or by any means (electronic, mechanical, photocopying, recording or
otherwise) without the prior written permission of Nosy Crow Ltd.

A CIP catalogue record for this book is available from the British Library.

Printed in China
Papers used by Nosy Crow are made from wood grown
in sustainable forests.

1 3 5 7 9 8 6 4 2

GO WILD
AT THE
SEASIDE

GOLDIE HAWK & RACHAEL SAUNDERS

nosy crow

NOTE TO GROWN-UPS

Grown-ups, be warned: this book contains large waves, sharp rocks and dangerous sea creatures.

'What?!' we hear you say . . .

But we believe it's important to teach children how to enjoy everything nature has to offer with due care. Along with our instructions, we've included plenty of reminders about safety. We know that you will supervise your children properly when engaging in any potentially dangerous activities, but we also hope that this book will encourage you to join in and rediscover the fun and magic of going

WILD AT THE SEASIDE!

The sea is mysterious, wild and beautiful, with amazing creatures from toxic sea slugs to velvet swimming crabs. Here you will discover plants and creatures of every colour of the rainbow. Perhaps you'll explore a cave or build a boat from driftwood, or play some beach games with your family and friends. Whatever you do, I hope this book helps you love our seas and everything in them even more.

GWEN POTTER — NATIONAL TRUST COUNTRYSIDE MANAGER

CONTENTS

ARE YOU READY TO GO WILD AT THE SEASIDE?

Do you love adventure, getting outdoors and making a splash? Are you *shore*? Then this is the book for you!

In this ultimate guide, you will find lots of fun activities to do at the seaside, from exploring rock pools and tracking seabirds, to building a sand sculpture and going surfing. You will also learn exactly what not to do, from getting caught in a rip current to standing on a sea urchin.

This book is about being safe and having fun. But it's also about having adventures. You should be willing to get a bit sandy and wet and you absolutely MUST be good at working in a team.

There are three important rules for going wild at the seaside:

1. When in doubt, DON'T!
2. Always ask your grown-up
3. Have fun!

Are you ready for your beach adventure to begin?
Then . . . **LET'S GO WILD!**

TOP TIP
Stick with your grown-up and never push anyone into doing something they don't feel comfortable with!

PLANNING YOUR SEASIDE ADVENTURE

The key to having the best seaside adventure is planning your trip well. To do this, you need to know about the times of the tides.

The sea is at different levels at different times of the day. It rises and falls twice a day as the positions of the Moon, the Earth and the Sun change. When it's high tide, the water level rises and floods the beach. When it's low tide, the water level falls and leaves the beach.

When the Sun and Moon are in line with each other, pulling in the same direction, there is a strong 'spring tide'. When the Sun and Moon pull in opposite directions, there is a weaker 'neap tide'.

It's always important to check the tide times. If you don't, you might set off for your seaside adventure to discover there is no beach to walk on. Or you might be halfway through a rock pool safari and suddenly realise you are surrounded by water and can't get back to the shore!

The best time to go is at low tide, when you can explore the whole beach.

TOP TIP
A 'spring tide' has nothing to do with spring. Both spring tides and neap tides happen all year round.

You can check the tide times online at **www.metoffice.gov.uk/ public/weather/tide-times.**

DIFFERENT KINDS OF BEACHES

There are lots of different kinds of beach, and different creatures can be found in each type of beach habitat. Which kind of beach will you explore?

SANDY BEACH

Sand is made from tiny pieces of broken-up rock and shell that have been worn down by the sea over millions of years.

BEST FOR:
building sandcastles, sand surfing, paddling barefoot and finding razor shells.

WORST FOR:
rock-climbing, having a tidy picnic, building a pebble arch.

DID YOU KNOW?
The white sand on tropical beaches is made from the crushed skeletons of coral polyps and the poo of parrotfish!

SHINGLE BEACH

Shingle beaches are filled with small to medium-sized rounded pebbles and stones, sometimes called 'cobbles'. You can also often find sea glass or 'lucky glass' as some people call it, which are pieces of glass that have been smoothed by the sea.

BEST FOR:
collecting interesting pebbles or sea glass, spotting shorebirds, building pebble arches.

WORST FOR:
skimboarding, barefoot exploring, playing beach cricket.

ROCKY BEACH

Rocky beaches are often filled with interesting rock pools and large rocks covered in molluscs such as mussels and barnacles.

BEST FOR:
climbing, rock pooling, exploring caves.

WORST FOR:
building sandcastles, digging holes, comfy sunbathing.

DID YOU KNOW?
The rocks on a rocky beach can range from thousands to BILLIONS of years old!

DIFFERENT BEACH ZONES

When scientists study beaches, they often talk about different beach 'zones' or habitats.

SPLASH ZONE

This part of the beach is always uncovered and only gets splashed by waves at high tide. There are few sea creatures to be found here, but a lot of plants, such as lyme grass and sea spurge.

STRANDLINE

Between the upper zone and the splash zone is the strandline, sometimes also called the seaweed line. Here, you can find seaweed, shells, jellyfish, fish skeletons and driftwood that have been washed up or 'stranded' by the high tide.

UPPER ZONE
Sometimes this zone is underwater, but only at very high tide or during spring tides. You might find rocks covered with seaweed, barnacles or periwinkles on them, and the odd crab.

MIDDLE ZONE
The sea covers this zone during high tide and uncovers it during low tide. In this zone, you can find creatures such as crabs, limpets and rocks covered in multicoloured seaweeds.

LOWER ZONE
This part of the beach is usually covered in water, but at very low tides you can explore it. This is where you will find the highest number of creatures, from fish and mussels to sea anemones and starfish.

WHAT YOU WILL NEED AT THE SEASIDE
THE ULTIMATE SEASIDE EXPLORER'S KIT

The ultimate seaside explorer needs the right gear: not too much or you won't be able to carry it; not too little or you won't be prepared.

WHAT TO TAKE:

- Notebook and pencil
- Bucket
- Clear container
- Fishing net
- Spade
- Magnifying glass
- Pair of binoculars
- Some string
- Torch
- Towel
- Tennis ball (or two)
- Cricket bat
- Snacks or a picnic
- Drinking water
- Mobile phone (for emergencies)
- Sun cream
- Bin liners for collecting rubbish
- First aid kit: bandages, antiseptic wipes, scissors, blister plasters, hydrocortisone cream

WHAT NOT TO TAKE:
unicycle, your pet hamster, lawnmower, bubble wrap.

WHAT TO WEAR:

- T-shirt
- Sunhat
- Shorts or trousers
- Warm jumper
- Swimming costume or trunks
- Wetsuit
- Old trainers, wellies or wetsuit boots

WHAT NOT TO WEAR:
shark costume, feather headdress, swanky suit, your grandma's precious pearls.

WHAT TO DO AT THE SEASIDE

GO ON A ROCK POOL SAFARI

Rock pools, or 'tide pools', are pools of seawater brought in by the tide that get stuck in the rocks when the tide goes back out. They might look like magical places to live for a sea creature, but life in a rock pool can actually be very tough. When the tide goes out, the water starts to dry out and becomes very salty. If it dries out too much, sea creatures unable to escape from the pool can die. That's why the rock pools closest to the water have the most life, because sea will be coming in to cover them the most often.

DID YOU KNOW?
It can take years for seaweed to grow on rocks. So DON'T yank it out!

Have a look inside the rock pool. What can you see near the surface? And what's down at the bottom? Lift any rocks gently and spot what's hiding underneath. Don't forget to put them back when you've finished looking.

Dip your hands into the pool and see what you can catch. Put each creature into a bucket of seawater straight away and return it to where you found it before you catch another one.

Note down all of the creatures and wildlife you find in your notebook, and don't forget to draw a picture too!

WHAT YOU MIGHT FIND IN A ROCK POOL:
· crabs
· little fish such as gobies and blennies
· shells
· prawns or shrimps
· mussels

WHAT YOU WON'T FIND IN A ROCK POOL:
· blue whale
· shark
· microwave
· treasure chest (unless you're very lucky!)

REMEMBER
Be careful if you're using a fishing net — small creatures can get tangled up and injured in it.

CATCH A CRAB

The best time to go crabbing is just as the tide is beginning to rise because crabs bury themselves in the sand when the tide is going out. Crabs love to hide near piers and harbour walls – so these are great places to try and catch one. Be careful not to fall in!

YOU WILL NEED:

some bait, such as a mussel or a tiny bit of raw bacon; a small weight, such as a stone; some string; a fishing net and a clear container filled with seawater.

1. Tie the weight and bait to your string.

2. Drop this into the water and lower it down until you can feel it touching the bottom.

3. If you feel a tug, carefully pull your string back up.

4. Use your fishing net to catch your crab.

5. Place your crab in a container full of seawater to get a better look.

6. To identify what kind of crab you've caught, go to pages 60–61.

WARNING
Never put two crabs in one bucket as they may fight!

Be careful when picking up a crab. Hold it on either side of its shell with your thumb and middle finger.

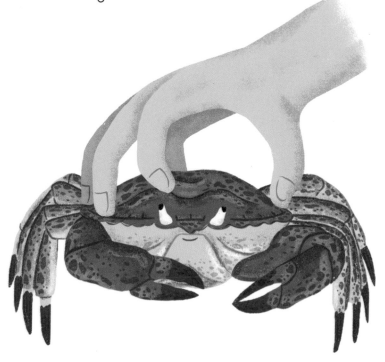

When you've finished inspecting your crab, don't forget to return it to where you found it.

BUILD A PEBBLE ARCH

Why not try a spot of beach engineering by building a pebble arch?

1. Collect your pebbles – you want a variety of sizes, from smaller pebbles to larger stones. You'll find it much easier to build your arch using flatter pebbles and stones than round ones!

2. Find a level spot on the beach and place the largest rocks about 30 cm apart.

3. Starting on one side, begin stacking your pebbles in a slanted tower, holding on to them so that they stay in place. Use smaller pebbles towards the top or centre of your arch.

4. Once you reach the top of your arch, start building downwards again, angling your stones towards the other base rock. You will need a friend (or two!) to help you hold the first side and top of the arch in place.

5. Once all your stones are in place, your arch should stand in place without your support!

You can also try to create a balance sculpture. See how many pebbles or stones you can balance on top of each other without them toppling over.

DID YOU KNOW?
The Rock Stacking World Championship is held each year at the Llano Earth Art Festival in Texas, USA.

BUILD AN ENORMOUS SANDCASTLE

The key to building an enormous sandcastle is using the right sand. It needs to be wet enough that it sticks together, so you can mould and carve it into shapes.

1. Dig sand with your spade and pile it up in a big heap to create your castle foundations. Then add extra seawater, using your bucket, and pat the sand down.

2. Now add towers and turrets by filling your bucket with sand, adding water, and quickly turning your bucket over on top of your castle foundations.

3. Once you have finished adding towers and turrets, decorate your sandcastle with shells, interesting stones, sea glass and old seaweed from the strandline.

MAKE A SAND SCULPTURE

Sand sculpting is a serious business. To make your sculpture, it might be a good idea to draw a sketch of what you'd like to create first.

TEN THINGS TO SCULPT:

1. sea monster
2. giant treasure chest
3. boat
4. dolphin
5. mermaid
6. dog
7. enormous ice-cream
8. dragon
9. car
10. your favourite book character!

DID YOU KNOW?
In 2008, sand sculptors in Dorset, England, built a hotel including two beds, a sofa and more, all from sand.

DIG A REALLY BIG HOLE

Enjoy digging? Why not dig a really big hole?

As you dig, make a note of the creatures you find. Small creatures, razor shells and crabs all burrow into the sand.

And don't forget to keep an eye out for buried treasure (yes, really!). You might be lucky enough to find some old Victorian pennies, dropped long ago during a holiday to the seaside, or even some antique jewellery.

REMEMBER
Always fill your hole with sand again before you leave, or you could injure someone!

DO:
make up your own digging songs, take regular water breaks, bury yourself up to the knees and see how long it takes to escape!

DON'T:
dig a hole deeper than waist height. If the sand collapses you could get stuck or hurt.

SEASIDE FACTS

1. The longest natural beach, at 120 km (74.5 miles) long, is called Cox's Bazar in southern Bangladesh.

2. A blue whale can eat 40 million krill each day.

3. Each dolphin has their own unique whistle that makes them recognisable to other dolphins.

4. Puffins keep the same mate for life and they say hello to their mate by rubbing bills, performing funny dances and bowing to each other.

5. Fish have been around for more than 450 million years — that's more than twice as long as mammals.

6. The biggest crab is called a Japanese spider crab and it is half as long as a London bus from the end of one leg to another!

7. An adult seal can hold its breath for at least half an hour.

8. In 1992, a cargo ship accidentally dropped 29,000 plastic bath toys into the Pacific Ocean. Fifteen years later, yellow ducks, blue turtles and green frogs started washing up on beaches all over the world!

9. Giant squid have eyes that are as big as footballs.

10. It's easier to float on the water in the Red Sea, which lies between Africa and Asia, because the water is so salty.

MAKE YOUR OWN KITE
YOU WILL NEED:

two thin bamboo sticks or wooden dowels from a DIY shop or garden centre (one around 70 cm, the other around 60 cm long – ask a grown-up to help if they need cutting to size); one ball of string; large sheet of brown paper or wrapping paper (70 cm x 100 cm); pencil or pen; scissors; strong sticky tape; paint, ribbons, stickers or other decorations.

1. Mark a line two thirds of the way along the longest stick. Now mark a line halfway along your shorter stick or dowel. Place the short stick horizontally over the longer stick so it makes a cross shape.

2. Attach the sticks using your string.

3. Take your string and loop it around the end of one stick, tying a tight knot. Then stretch your string around the other three corners, tying it to each end and securing with sticky tape as you go along. Now you have your diamond-shaped frame!

4. Place your frame on the brown paper and draw a line around the kite, adding a 3 cm margin.

5. Cut out this shape and fold the paper over your frame, securing it with sticky tape.

6. Attach a piece of string from one end of your cross stick (the horizontal stick) to the other. Then tie a piece of string to the middle of this line. This piece needs to be very long as it will be the line your kite flies from.

7. Now you can add a tail to your kite and decorate it with paint, ribbons, stickers or whatever else you want!

23

FLY YOUR KITE

To fly your kite, you will need a nice, windy spot on the beach. This is easiest done with the help of a friend.

1. Ask your friend to hold the kite.

2. Unwind your kite string. At the same time, walk away from your friend, with your back to the wind.

3. Once your string is fully unwound and pulled tight, ask your friend to launch your kite by throwing it upwards and letting the wind blow it up into the sky. Sometimes it helps to run backwards while pulling on the string to get extra lift.

WARNING
Don't fly your kite next to a tree, a power line or close to a road!

GO SAND SURFING

Some beaches have big sand dunes, which are created when wind from the sea blows sand up the beach.

To go sand surfing, you need a sand dune without too much grass. You also need something to slide down the dune on. A bodyboard is perfect, but you could also use a skimboard. Wear goggles to protect your eyes.

Jump on your board and slide down the sand dune. To steer, lean your body to the right or the left.

REMEMBER
Don't sand surf near grass or plants, as you could damage the wildlife living there.

GO EXPLORING ON A KAYAK

Some parts of the seaside you can't explore on foot very easily. That's where a kayak comes in handy! All you need is a kayak, a life jacket and a helmet, a grown-up and a calm area of sea – you don't want big waves or a strong current or you might end up capsizing.

1. Carefully get into your kayak – try hard not to fall in.

2. Hold your paddle with a light grip, so that your knuckles are in line with the blades.

3. Move along by dipping your paddle into the water on your right side and pushing the water back behind you, then do the same on your left side.

DO:
stay close to land, listen to your grown-up, make sure your life jacket and helmet fit properly.

DON'T:
whack a seagull with your oar, take a nap or do the hokey-cokey.

4. If you want to veer left, paddle more on your right side; if you want to veer right, paddle more on your left.

GO BODYBOARDING

1. Paddle out with your bodyboard – make sure the wrist strap is attached (you don't want the board to blow or float away!).

2. Once the water is waist deep and you've spotted a good wave to catch, turn your board so that you are facing the beach. Then, kick with your feet so that you're moving and keep looking backwards so you can see the wave coming.

3. If you catch the wave, it should push you towards the beach . . . smile and enjoy the ride!

4. If you don't catch the wave, keep trying! It may take some practice.

TOP TIP
Don't go out of your depth, so if you fall off your board you can stand up easily.

GO SURFING

Surfing is a bit trickier than bodyboarding, and you might need to take a lesson or two before you catch a wave!

1. Lie on the board so that your toes are over the edge, your body is in the centre of the board and your hands are paddling in the water.

2. Paddle out to where the waves are breaking. Start with the shallow waves first. Once you find your wave, turn around so that you're facing the shore and start paddling and kicking, turning your head to check how far away the wave is.

3. Once you feel yourself being moved by the wave, place your hands on the board, level with your chest, then jump up so that you're standing with one foot forwards and one backwards. To balance more easily, hold your arms out.

4. If you don't catch the wave or you fall in, don't worry! This is perfectly normal, and it can take lots of practice before you get the hang of it.

DID YOU KNOW?
The most people to ever stand on one surfboard is 47!

LEARN SOME SURFING LINGO

What's this surfer saying?

Dude, I was shredding this gnarly wave, totally locked in, when I saw a Barney in the water and had to bail before I majorly wiped out!

Ankle busters/snappers: small waves
Bail: to jump off your board to avoid a wipe out!
Barney: a beginner surfer
Carve: a sharp turn
Gnarly: particularly dangerous surfing conditions
Hang ten: have all toes on the front (nose) of the board
Lip/crest: the top part where a wave is about to break
Locked in: surfing in the tube of a wave
Noodled: tired
Quasimodo: to surf in a hunched-up position
Shredding: aggressive surfing
Stuffed: pushed underwater by a wave
Wipe out: to fall off the board when you're surfing

GO SKIMBOARDING

Skimboarding is a bit like surfing, but over the sand on a very thin layer of water and on a thinner, shorter board.

You can only skimboard on sandy beaches – if you try this on shingle beaches, you probably won't get very far and your skimboard will just get scratched.

1. Wait for a small wave to wash up at the shore.
2. As the wave starts to wash back out, hold your board flat to one side of your body and start running with it.
3. Let your board go and it should slide along the thin layer of water, parallel to the sea.
4. Now for the tricky bit – jump on to the board with one foot at the front and one at the back.
5. If you don't fall off, bend your knees slightly and enjoy the ride!

GO PADDLEBOARDING

WHAT TO WEAR:
sun cream, swimwear,
life jacket.

WHAT NOT TO WEAR:
snorkel, ski wear,
jeans, top hat.

A paddleboard looks a bit like a surfboard but it's longer and heavier, with a grippy bit to stand on.

Balancing on a paddleboard might take a bit of practice, so start on your knees. Unlike a kayak oar, paddleboard oars usually only have one paddle end, but steering is still the same.

Paddle on the right side if you want to veer left, and left side if you want to veer right.

When you're feeling more confident on your board, carefully stand up and continue paddling. Try not to fall in!

REMEMBER
Paddleboarding is difficult if there are waves, so only go if it's calm.

GO SNORKELLING

To go snorkelling, you will need a mask, a snorkel and, if you can find them, some flippers.

To use your snorkel, place the mouthpiece in your mouth and bite down so that no water can come through. Now you'll be able to breathe while looking underwater. Don't swim down too deep, though, or air won't be able to get through your snorkel.

TOP TIP
Flippers are hard to walk in. Put them on by the water and walk backwards into the sea.

GO SAILING

There are lots of different sailing boats, but the best type to start sailing on is a small dinghy.

PARTS OF A DINGHY

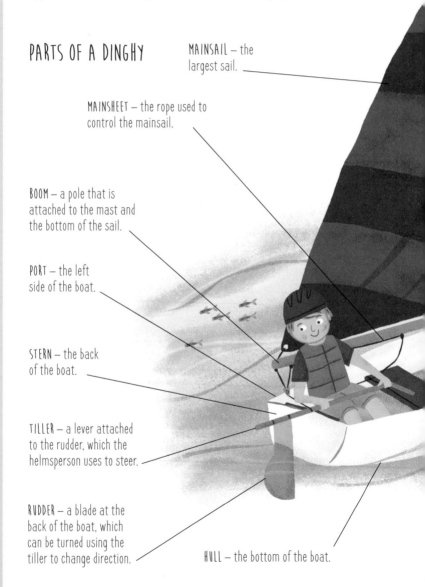

MAINSAIL – the largest sail.

MAINSHEET – the rope used to control the mainsail.

BOOM – a pole that is attached to the mast and the bottom of the sail.

PORT – the left side of the boat.

STERN – the back of the boat.

TILLER – a lever attached to the rudder, which the helmsperson uses to steer.

RUDDER – a blade at the back of the boat, which can be turned using the tiller to change direction.

HULL – the bottom of the boat.

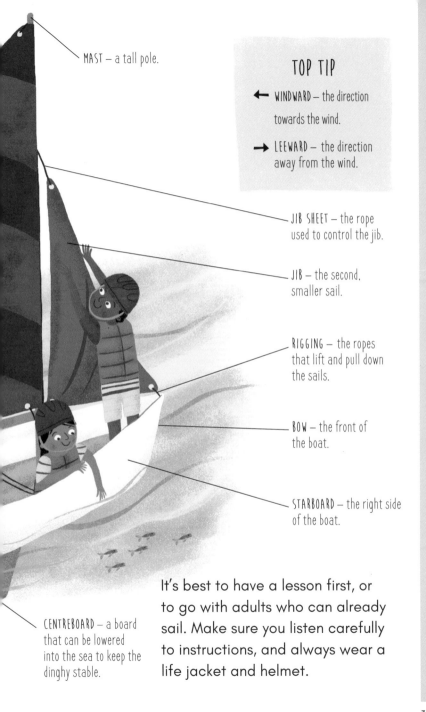

MAST – a tall pole.

TOP TIP

← WINDWARD – the direction towards the wind.

→ LEEWARD – the direction away from the wind.

JIB SHEET – the rope used to control the jib.

JIB – the second, smaller sail.

RIGGING – the ropes that lift and pull down the sails.

BOW – the front of the boat.

STARBOARD – the right side of the boat.

CENTREBOARD – a board that can be lowered into the sea to keep the dinghy stable.

It's best to have a lesson first, or to go with adults who can already sail. Make sure you listen carefully to instructions, and always wear a life jacket and helmet.

SAILING BASICS

1. Decide who is the helmsperson (the person steering) and who is the crew (the person/people in the boat), although some small boats are designed to be sailed by just one person.

2. The helmsperson should get in the boat first, while the crew pushes it out from the shore and jumps in once the boat is moving.

3. Push the centreboard down once you're out of shallow water.

4. The wind should hit the sails as you set off and push the boat along.

5. To steer, push the tiller in the opposite direction to the way you want to turn.

6. To turn, you can either 'tack' (if you are sailing into the wind) or 'jibe' (if the wind is behind you). Before you do either, the helmsperson must warn the crew because the boom will swing around as the sail moves (and might knock you out of the boat)!

PLAY BOULES

Boules is a French game, also known as *pétanque*, but it was originally played by the ancient Greeks. Traditionally, you need special boules balls to play – but you can also play this game with some tennis balls and a stone.

1. Get into teams and pick your balls.
2. Draw a starting circle in the sand. This is where you will all throw the balls from.
3. Someone throws the jack or stone.
4. Everyone takes it in turn to throw their balls, aiming for their ball to stop as close to the jack or stone as possible.

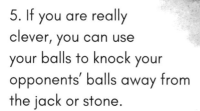

5. If you are really clever, you can use your balls to knock your opponents' balls away from the jack or stone.

6. When everyone has thrown their balls, go and take a closer look at where all the balls have landed.

7. Whoever's ball is the closest to the jack or stone wins.

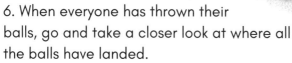

BONJOUR!

Why not try playing your game of boules while speaking French? Here are some useful words:

le terrain: the patch of ground where boules is played

le but/le cochonnet: the target (or piglet!)

le cercle/le rond: the throwing circle

on fait une partie?: shall we have a game?

oui, bien sûr: yes, certainly.

bien joué: well played!

SKIM STONES

Skimming stones is a great game to play at the seaside, but you do need calm water — the more waves, the trickier the skim! When you skim a stone, the aim is to throw it in a way that makes it skip or bounce across the water. The more skips, the more impressive the skim!

First of all, find yourself the perfect stone or pebble. It needs to be thin, flat, palm-sized and very light.

REMEMBER
Don't skim stones
if there are any birds
(or any people)
in the water!

1. Hold the stone with your strongest hand, so that the stone is on top of your middle finger and underneath your thumb and forefinger.
2. Bend your knees and look at the point you want to throw towards.
3. Throw the stone straight out towards the water with as much force as you can manage and watch it skim. Use your thumb and forefinger to add spin as you throw.

It will take a bit of practice, but soon you'll be a champion skimmer!

SCORING CARD
0 skips: more practice needed
1–2 skips: good start
3–4 skips: impressive
5–6 skips: master at work
7+ skips: expert

COLLECT MUSSELS FOR DINNER

When the tide is out on clean, unpolluted beaches, you can collect mussels for a tasty meal.

TOP TIP
Don't collect mussels between May and August. This is when mussels breed.

Only take the best looking, shiniest shells from rocks as close to the sea as possible. A broken or cracked mussel might make you very ill! Remember, never collect mussels after it's been raining.

COOK MUSSELS FOR DINNER

First, put your mussels in a bucket of cold, salty water to soak overnight. Then, one by one, pull the beards off them and scrub them with a clean scrubbing brush. If you spot any opened mussels, tap them lightly on a hard surface. If they don't close, this means they're not safe to eat!

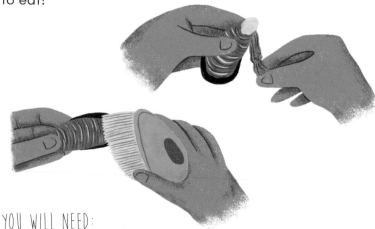

YOU WILL NEED:

mussels; large saucepan; olive oil or butter; a chopped shallot; two cloves of garlic; juice of a lemon.

1. Find a large pan and add one tablespoon of olive oil or butter, one chopped shallot, two cloves of crushed garlic and the juice of one lemon. Cook these ingredients for a few minutes with the help of your grown-up.

WARNING
If a mussel shell doesn't open as it cooks, DO NOT try to eat it. You will really regret it a few hours later!

2. Drain the mussels and then pour them into the saucepan with your other ingredients. Now leave to cook with a lid on for six minutes on a medium heat, giving the pan a shake every now and then.

3. When your mussels are done, all the shells will have opened. Serve them with a sprinkle of parsley and some bread to soak up all the yummy broth.

GO FISHING

The best spot for fishing in the sea is somewhere safe and quiet — you don't want to be swept away by a wave or catch any people swimming! Some beaches are protected, so always make sure you have permission to fish first.

1. Cast your line by bringing the rod to your side and then swinging it smoothly in the direction you want to fish in.

2. Wait quietly — fish are startled by loud noises, so don't be tempted to sing or put a radio on!

3. If you feel or see the rod jerk, you might have a bite — reel or pull the line back in and see what you've caught.

4. If you don't feel a bite after 10–15 minutes, take your line in and cast it again.

Fishing takes a lot of practice, but keep at it and you'll soon be *reelly* good!

REMEMBER
Anyone over the age of 12 will need a rod licence. Find out more at www.gov.uk/fishing-licences.

EXPLORE A CAVE

Some beaches have caves at the shore. These are created by crashing waves, which wear away, or 'erode', the rocky headland.

Be careful when you're exploring your cave — take a grown-up and make sure you remember to bring a torch.

Once inside, make a noise and wait to hear the echo! What can you see?

YOU MIGHT FIND:
bats, spiders, rock pools, crabs.

YOU PROBABLY WON'T FIND:
trolls, cavemen, a brass band (but you never know)!

WARNING
Make sure you check the tide times so the sea doesn't come in and trap you in the cave!

REMEMBER
Only collect small pieces of driftwood – the bigger pieces can provide homes for beetles.

COLLECT DRIFTWOOD

Driftwood is wood that was floating in the sea and has been washed up on the beach. It often has little holes in it made by tiny wood-eating animals.

The best times for driftwood hunting are at low tide or after a storm, when the sea has washed it up.

There are all sorts of things you can do with driftwood. You can:
• craft it into a boat (see next page)
• use it as a piece of furniture
• create a dream-catcher.

MAKE A DRIFTWOOD BOAT

First, you need a good chunk of driftwood to make the main body of your boat. It should be long and slim with a flat bottom so that it doesn't topple over in the water.

Next, find a long, thin stick for your mast. Ask a grown-up to help you cut a hole in the centre of your driftwood (but don't go all the way through) and slot your mast into the hole so that it stands up by itself.

Find some washed-up seaweed for your sails. Tie one end to the top of your mast and one to the bow (front) of the boat.

Now your boat is complete, why not launch it in the water? You could even have a boat race!

PLAY BEACH VOLLEYBALL

To play beach volleyball, you need a group of friends, a large ball (an inflatable beach ball will do) and a net held up by two sticks. If you don't have a net, you can just draw a line in the sand where the net would be.

The aim is to keep the ball off the ground on your side of the court and to make it hit the ground on the other side of the court, without hitting the net (or line in the sand).

1. Create your court by drawing a large rectangle in the sand and set up your net (or draw your line in the sand) at the halfway point.

2. Get into two even teams, one team on each side of the net.

3. One of the teams starts by serving the ball. Players on the same team can bounce the ball to each other before hitting it over the net.

4. If you manage to make the ball hit the sand on the other side of the net, your team wins a point.

5. If you make the ball hit the net or if you miss the ball and it lands in the sand (or the sea!), the other team wins a point.

PLAY BEACH CRICKET

YOU WILL NEED:
• cricket bat
• tennis ball or two
• wickets, made of sticks of driftwood
• clear area of beach

1. Decide who will start as the batsman and bowler. Everyone else are the fielders and stand around the pitch, waiting to catch the ball.

2. Mark out the far end of your pitch in the sand. This is where the batsman will run to.

3. The batsman stands in front of the wicket. The bowler bowls the ball to the batsman.

4. If the batsman misses and the ball hits the wicket, the batsman is out. If any of the fielders catch the ball, the batsman is out. The batsman is also out if they hit the ball into the sea!

5. If the batsman hits the ball (and if no fielders have caught it), they need to run to the other end of the pitch and back again. Don't forget to count how many runs the batsman makes before the fielders get the ball back to the bowler.

PLAY FRISBEE

Frisbee is a fun game to play in pairs or in a group. All you need is . . . a frisbee!

TO THROW A FRISBEE

1. Point your shoulder in the direction that you would like to throw.

2. Hold the frisbee with your fingers on the curve of the frisbee and your thumb on the top.

3. Bring your frisbee towards your chest by bending your arm. Keep the frisbee horizontal and flat.

4. Now straighten your arm and throw the frisbee towards your friend.

EXPLORE A BEACH AT DUSK

A lot of beach wildlife only comes out at night, from barn owls hunting for mice, to seals and dolphins swimming in the sea. Don't forget your torch, and keep an eye out for holes in the sand!

If it's a clear night, look up at the stars and see if you can spot any constellations or shooting stars.

WHAT TO SEE AT THE SEASIDE

There's so much for you to spot at the seaside if you look carefully. So pick up your binoculars or magnifying glass and get exploring!

FISH

BLENNY can often be found hiding between stones, looking for worms and molluscs to eat. They have a long dorsal (back) fin and fat lips.

GOBY are very good at covering themselves with sand to hide. They can be transparent or brightly coloured, with two dorsal (back) fins and large eyes.

BUTTERFISH can be found in seaweed or between rocks. They are long and slippery with brownish-black bodies and black spots.

CLINGFISH are orangey-red fish that have a triangular head and strong fins and suckers, which they use to stick to rocks.

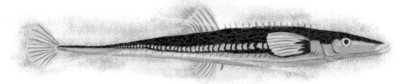

SEA STICKLEBACK are small, long fish, with 15 sharp spines on their backs to protect them against predators.

CRUSTACEANS

PRAWNS AND SHRIMP are small with a protective shell and can swim very quickly.

LOBSTERS have eight legs and two large, powerful claws, which are used for defence and for eating their food.

CRABS

There are lots of different types of crab, but all have 10 legs including a set of claws and pincers.

SHORE CRABS are very common and have brown, orange or green shells.

HAIRY CRABS look like shore crabs but with hairy legs and a hairy shell.

HERMIT CRABS make their homes from empty sea shells.

VELVET CRABS have red eyes and are covered with hair. They eat other crabs and might give you a nasty nip.

EDIBLE CRABS have an orange, oval-shaped shell and long, black-tipped claws.

SEA MAMMALS AND SHARKS

COMMON SEALS have a thick layer of blubber that keeps them warm. They can be spotted swimming in the sea or resting on rocks. Don't get too close, though – they can bite.

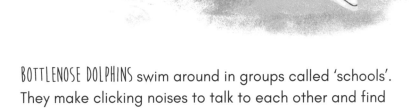

BOTTLENOSE DOLPHINS swim around in groups called 'schools'. They make clicking noises to talk to each other and find their prey, and they love to play around boats.

HARBOUR PORPOISES
look a bit like dolphins but with a rounder nose. They also swim around in schools and come to the surface for air, although they don't jump high like dolphins.

SHARKS that you might see in the UK are unlikely to be dangerous, but you might come across some basking sharks. They are grey-coloured and have tiny eyes and a huge mouth, which they keep open to catch small fish and plankton.

HUMPBACK WHALES are enormous with a bumpy snout and very large flippers. They sing to communicate. Every so often, they jump out of the water and dive back in – this is called 'breaching'.

SMALLER SEA CREATURES

DID YOU KNOW?
If a starfish's arm
is bitten off, it
can regrow!

COMMON STARFISH have five arms but no head, eyes or brain. A starfish can see by raising the tips of its tentacles, which are light-sensitive.

SEAHORSES are one of the slowest swimmers in the world. They have long, thin snouts, which allow them to find food in small nooks and crannies.

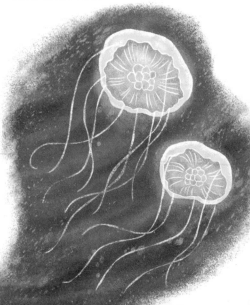

JELLYFISH are almost entirely made of water. Some have tentacles that can sting if you touch them.

SEA URCHINS have a
round shell called a
'test', which is covered
in sharp, poisonous
spines.

ANEMONES look like plants and can often be very colourful.
They use their poisonous tentacles to paralyse prey,
before pulling it into their stomach.

SEA CUCUMBERS are slug-like animals that come in all kinds
of different colours. If it is attacked, a sea cucumber will
squirt out its sticky guts.

MOLLUSCS

OCTOPUSES have eight arms with two rows of suckers, which they use to catch and eat food. They have three hearts, are very intelligent and can solve tricky problems, like opening jars and using tools.

SQUID are very quick swimmers and can change colour. They have a tube-shaped, bag-like body, with two long tentacles, which they use to catch food, and eight arms lined with suckers.

SEA SNAILS look similar to the snails you might find in your garden, but they have gills and live in the water.

DOG WHELKS are usually white, spiral-shelled molluscs that hunt other animals in rock pools. They can drill through the shells of other animals to eat them.

MUSSELS are a bluish-black colour and they cling to rocks or the bottom of boats with a special beard-like thread.

BARNACLES are tiny shellfish that swim for a short time after hatching, before attaching themselves to rocks, boats and even whales.

BIRDS

HERRING GULLS are white and grey birds, with webbed feet for paddling in the water and long pink legs for wading.

GANNETS are large, white birds with black wing tips, a long pointed bill and a yellow head.

LITTLE TERNS are grey and white seabirds. They have a black mask around their eyes like a bandit.

PUFFINS are black and white birds with colourful beaks. They build nests in underground burrows.

CORMORANTS are large and black with white cheeks. They are excellent fishers and have a specially designed neck for diving into the sea at high speeds.

CURLEWS are large birds with a very long, down-curved bill, long blue legs and greyish-brown bodies.

OYSTERCATCHERS have bright red legs. Some have blunt beaks to 'hammer' shells, while others have 'cutting' beaks that are better at snipping shells open.

LAPWINGS have a recognisable wispy black crest on their heads. They have dark green backs with flecks of purple and copper, and a white underside.

SANDPIPERS have long legs to walk through the water. Like many other waders, the tips of their beaks can feel the vibrations of their food moving in the sand.

SANDERLINGS are white with brown or grey backs and jet-black legs. You might spot them running along the water's edge on the hunt for washed-up fish to eat.

TURNSTONES are a chestnut-brown and black colour, with a black and white head. They get their name because they turn stones over to find food.

GUILLEMOTS have a dark brown body and a white chest. They look a bit like penguins, and gather on cliffs to lay their eggs.

TRACKING BIRD FOOTPRINTS
Match the bird to the footprint:

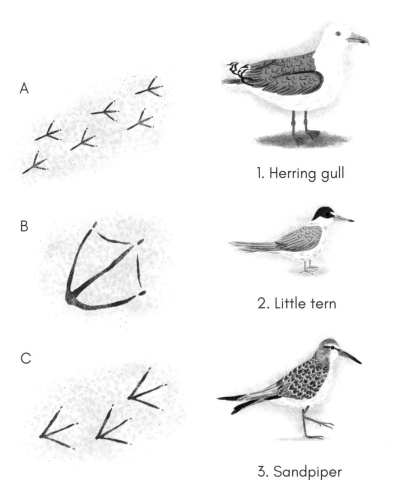

A

1. Herring gull

B

2. Little tern

C

3. Sandpiper

Answers: 1. B 2. A 3. C

SHELLS

A shell you find on the beach was once the home of a mollusc or a sea snail; and might again become the home of a small creature such as a hermit crab.

COMMON WHELK SHELLS are yellowish-brown and cone-shaped, with a spiral pattern.

OYSTER SHELLS are oval or pear-shaped with a rough, brownish-grey outside and a smooth white inside. Oysters are an expensive delicacy and are eaten raw.

SCALLOP SHELLS are very pretty and fan-shaped, varying from white to pink in colour. Scallops are often cooked and eaten by people.

COMMON COCKLE SHELLS are pale brown or grey, with a ribbed texture and white insides. They are very easy to find in the UK.

RAZOR SHELLS get their name because they look like an old-fashioned 'straight razor', which men used to shave their beards.

COMMON PERIWINKLE SHELLS are brown and spiral-shaped with a sharp point and a white lip. They were once homes to sea snails.

TURBAN TOP SHELLS look a bit like spinning tops and can be yellow, purple, white, brown or grey, often with patterns.

COWRIE SHELLS are small, pinky-brown shells that were once homes to sea snails. They can occasionally be found below rocks and cliffs and on shingle beaches.

WILDLIFE

Seaweed is a type of algae that grows on rocks and gets its energy from the sun. In places like Japan and Wales, seaweed is a common food to eat . . . but it has to be a certain type of seaweed, prepared in a special way, so do your homework if you want to forage your own!

DID YOU KNOW?
Sea belt can predict the weather. If it's dry and crisp, this means warm weather is due, but if it's wet and wilting, this means it's about to rain!

There are many different types of seaweed, but here are some you might spot during your trip to the seaside:

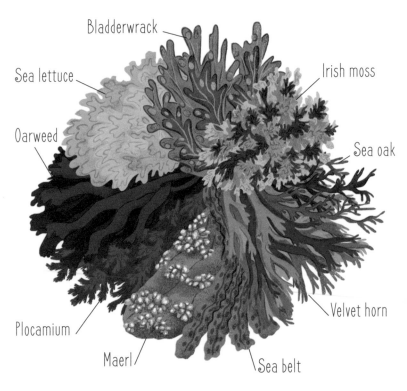

Bladderwrack

Sea lettuce

Irish moss

Oarweed

Sea oak

Plocamium

Velvet horn

Maerl

Sea belt

OTHER PLANTS TO SPOT

THRIFT gets its name because its flowers are very good at saving up water, and a 'thrifty' person is someone who is very good at saving up money.

MARRAM GRASS can be found on sand dunes and copes well in the wind and salty air.

SEA HOLLY can be found on sand and shingle beaches. It has prickly green leaves and blue flowers.

SEA KALE has pretty white flowers and cabbage-like green leaves.

SEA MILKWORT is a creeping plant with pretty pink flowers and green leaves.

BIRD'S FOOT TREFOIL grows on cliffs or grassy banks and has yellow and red flowers, so it sometimes gets the nickname 'bacon and eggs'.

SAVE YOUR SEASIDE

Let's face it, beaches are utterly rubbish when they're filled with rubbish. Not only do they look and smell much less pleasant, but all the animals, creatures and wildlife that live on or around them can be badly harmed or even killed by what we leave behind.

The bad news is that the amount of plastic in the ocean and on our coasts keeps rising, and plastic lasts an incredibly long time.

The good news is that you can do something to help during your trip to the beach. By spending just half an hour walking along the shore picking up rubbish, you could save a lot of lives.

Or, if you have more time, why not organise a full beach clean? You can start planning it a couple of weeks before your trip.

HOW TO ORGANISE A BEACH CLEAN

1. Check the tide times and organise the event at least two hours after a high tide.

2. If the beach is private, contact the beach owner. If the beach is public, contact the local council. They might even have bin liners and litter-pickers you can use.

3. Advertise for your beach clean in the days running up to it — you can create posters and let local shops or cafés know about it. You could even run a competition for the highest amount of rubbish found. Don't forget to let everyone know what they should bring with them — everyone will need gloves, bin bags in two colours (one for rubbish and one for recyclables) and, if you can find them, litter-pickers.

4. On the big day, wait for everyone to turn up before you begin cleaning. If you have lots of people with you, you can split up into two teams and start on different ends of the beach. If you have a smaller group, everyone can start on one side and move across the whole beach together.

5. As you walk along the beach, pick up rubbish and put it in the right bag.

6. At the end of your clean, count the number of recycling bags and rubbish bags.

SEASIDE SAFETY

SWIMMING IN THE SEA

Swimming in the sea can be great fun, but you absolutely must be careful, even if you're a strong swimmer. Always go with a grown-up and make sure you follow this checklist:

• only swim at a designated beach
• make sure you have permission to swim there
• never swim without your grown-up
• check that the beach has a lifeguard.

RIP CURRENTS

A rip current or rip tide is a very fast flow of water leading out to sea and it can be very strong. If you get caught in a rip current and it starts to sweep you out to sea, try to remain calm. If you panic and flap your arms, you'll waste all your energy and may even push yourself underwater. Take even breaths, remain floating, and try to swim sideways, parallel to the shore, until you have left the rip current. Then swim to the shoreline, while calmly calling for help.

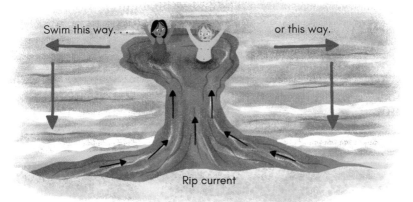

Swim this way. . . or this way.

Rip current

WILD WAVES

Waves can be wonderful to jump around in, but they can also be wild and unpredictable. If you're tumbled over in a wave, try to keep calm and float. It can feel like you're in a washing machine and that you'll never get back to the surface, but you will find your way back above the water soon enough. The best way to avoid being tumbled in a wave is to swim deep underneath it when it comes towards you.

SCARY TSUNAMIS

On rare occasions, an enormous series of waves called a 'tsunami' or a 'seismic sea wave' are created because of an earthquake or underwater landslide. These are highly unlikely to happen in the UK, but if you're on a beach abroad, it's good to know the signs:

• all of the water draws out of the beach or bay very quickly, leaving lots of fish and debris exposed on the beach
• frothing bubbles may appear at the surface of the sea
• you might hear a distant roar.

If you recognise these signs, you should leave the beach as soon as possible and get to higher land.

WHAT TO DO IF YOU GET STUNG BY A JELLYFISH

Jellyfish might look harmless, but can give you a nasty sting. If you do get stung, wash the area in seawater. Next, place the stung area in a bucket of warm water (you should be able to get some from a local café), or cover it with towels soaked in warm water. If the sting is mild, the symptoms should go after 30–90 minutes. But if you have chest pain or difficulty breathing, call for an ambulance.

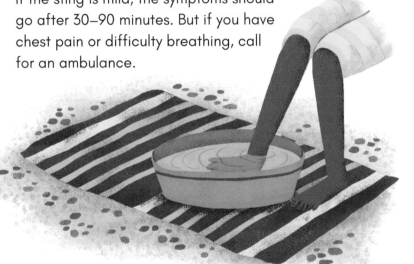

WHAT TO DO IF YOU STEP ON A WEEVER FISH

Weever fish lurk under the sand and, if you step on one, the spines on its back can pierce your skin and inject a poison. This is incredibly painful but, luckily, not lethal.

If you get stung by a weever fish, the best thing to do is to put your foot in a bucket filled with hot water and vinegar for 30–90 minutes and find a lifeguard or first aider to check the wound.

WHAT TO DO IF YOU STEP ON A SEA URCHIN

Sea urchins might look pretty amazing, but you won't be smiling if you touch one. The urchin's spines can pierce through your skin and become infected. If you do step or fall on one, find someone to help you. You will need to remove any spine fragments. If this is tricky, use tweezers to get them out. Next, scrub the area with soap and fresh water. This might sting, but it's very important to stop the wound becoming infected. Then, bathe the skin in hot water for an hour to ease the pain and get rid of any remaining spines.

Keep checking on the wound. If it goes red and puffy or you start to feel unwell, it might be infected, and you should go to a doctor straight away.

WHAT TO DO IF YOU GET ATTACKED BY A SHARK

The chances are, you won't be attacked by a shark if you are swimming. But if you do find yourself swimming in very deep, shark-infested water and spot a shark, try to remain calm. Swim away as quickly and calmly as you can and try to get out of the water.

Try not to thrash around – the shark might think you're injured and an easy catch for lunch.

If you do get attacked, give the shark a firm punch on the nose, eyes or gills. This will frighten it away.

SEASIDE QUIZ

1. What is the technical word for the back of a dinghy?
    A) Port
    B) Stern
    C) Starboard

2. Which mollusc can solve tricky problems, like opening jars and using tools?
    A) Mussel
    B) Cuttlefish
    C) Octopus

3. What is the name that scientists use for the part of a beach where everything is washed up?
    A) Middle zone
    B) Splash zone
    C) Strandline

4. What is the white sand from tropical beaches made out of?
    A) Crushed skeletons of coral polyps and parrotfish poo
    B) Angel fish scales and chalk from clifftops
    C) Crushed-up rocks and rainbowfish bones

5. Which sea bird has a specially designed neck for diving into the sea at a very high speed?
    A) Pelican
    B) Gannet
    C) Cormorant

6. Which seaweed can predict the weather?
  A) Sea belt
  B) Bladderwrack
  C) Sea lettuce

7. What is the name for the weakest tide?
  A) Spring tide
  B) Feeble tide
  C) Neap tide

8. Which crab can give you a very nasty nip?
  A) Edible crab
  B) Velvet crab
  C) Hairy crab

9. Which sea creature has eyes as big as footballs?
  A) Colossal hermit crab
  B) Giant squid
  C) Great butterfish

10. Why can you float more easily in the Red Sea?
  A) Because there are fewer fish in the sea
  B) Because the water contains more oxygen
  C) Because the water contains more salt

ANSWERS: 1. Stern 2. Octopus 3. Strandline 4. Crushed skeletons of coral polyps and the poo of parrotfish 5. Cormorant 6. Sea belt 7. Neap tide 8. Velvet crab 9. Giant squid 10. Because the seawater contains more salt

SUPER SEASIDE

We hope you have a wonderful time at the seaside. It can be a magical place, whether you're watching a crab scuttle over the rocks or exploring a rocky inlet by kayak.

While it's great fun to go wild at the seaside, it's most important to be respectful of this beautiful space. That means following the rules, listening to your grown-ups and being careful not to disturb the environment. As the saying goes, you should leave only footprints and take only memories!

GLOSSARY

Blubber The thick layer of fat between the skin and the muscle of sea mammals (such as whales) that keeps them warm.

Bow The front part of a boat.

Centreboard A board that can be lowered into the sea to keep a dinghy stable.

Constellation A group of stars that form a pattern. Scientists have identified 88 constellations in the night sky.

Crustacean Animals that live in water and have a hard shell and two pairs of antennae.

Dinghy A small, open boat with a mast and sails.

Dorsal fin A thin flat fin on the back of some fish.

Driftwood Wood that has been washed up on a beach, shore or bank.

Dusk The time after sunset and just before night.

Erode Slowly wear away.

Helmsperson Person who steers a ship or boat.

Hull The bottom of a boat.

Hydrocortisone cream Medicine that reduces swelling and redness of skin after a sting or insect bite.

Jib The second, smaller sail on a dinghy or boat.

Jibe The action of turning a boat when the wind is behind you.

Leeward The direction away from the wind.

Life jacket A sleeveless vest that can keep a person afloat in water.

Mollusc Any animal that has a soft body, no spine, and is often covered with a shell. Many live in water.

Port The left-hand side of a boat.

Rudder A blade at the back of a boat, which can be turned using the tiller to change direction.

Tack The action of turning a boat when sailing into the wind.

Tiller A lever attached to a boat's rudder, used to steer.

Tsunami A long, very high sea wave caused by an earthquake or undersea landslide.

Saltwater Water that comes from a sea or ocean.

Sea mammals Mammals that rely on the ocean or sea for their survival (such as seals, dolphins and whales).

Starboard The right-hand side of a boat.

Windward The direction towards the wind.

INDEX